STAR BIOGRAPHIES

KHALID

WITHDRAW

KENNY ABDO

Fly!
An Imprint of Abdo Zoom
abdobooks.com

abdobooks.com

Published by Abdo Zoom, a division of ABDO, P.O. Box 398166, Minneapolis, Minnesota 55439. Copyright © 2019 by Abdo Consulting Group, Inc. International copyrights reserved in all countries. No part of this book may be reproduced in any form without written permission from the publisher. Fly!™ is a trademark and logo of Abdo Zoom.

Printed in the United States of America, North Mankato, Minnesota.
092018
012019

THIS BOOK CONTAINS
RECYCLED MATERIALS

Photo Credits: Alamy, AP Images, Shutterstock,
©Chris Pizzello p20 /Invision/AP/Shutterstock
Production Contributors: Kenny Abdo, Jennie Forsberg, Grace Hansen
Design Contributors: Dorothy Toth, Neil Klinepier

Library of Congress Control Number: 2018946253

Publisher's Cataloging-in-Publication Data

Names: Abdo, Kenny, author.
Title: Khalid / by Kenny Abdo.
Description: Minneapolis, Minnesota : Abdo Zoom, 2019 | Series: Star biographies
    | Includes online resources and index.
Identifiers: ISBN 9781532125454 (lib. bdg.) | ISBN 9781641856904 (pbk.) |
    ISBN 9781532126475 (ebook) | ISBN 9781532126987 (Read-to-me ebook)
Subjects: LCSH: Khalid, 1998- (Khalid Robinson)--Juvenile literature. | Singers--
    Biography--Juvenile literature. | Popular music--Juvenile literature. Classification:
DDC 782.42164092 [B]--dc23

TABLE OF CONTENTS

Khalid 4

Early Years 6

The Big Time 10

Legacy 18

Glossary 22

Online Resources 23

Index 24

KHALID

He may be young, however pop sensation Khalid is anything but dumb and broke.

Khalid has topped the music **charts**, received many awards, and sold out concerts in his short musical career.

EARLY YEARS

Khalid Robinson was born in Fort Stewart, Georgia, in 1998.

Tennessee

North Carolina

South Carolina

Alabama

GEORGIA

FORT STEWART

Florida

He has lived in many places because his mom was in the military. They lived in Kentucky, New York, and Germany.

They **settled** in El Paso, Texas, when Khalid was a junior in high school. There, he studied musical theater and singing. Khalid would write songs of his own and put them up on **SoundCloud** for people to hear.

THE BIG TIME

Khalid wrote and released the song "Location" in 2016, because he wanted to be **prom king**. On prom night he won the crown. Even better, Kylie Jenner played the song on her Snapchat. More than 30 million people listened.

"Location" reached the Top 10 on Billboard's Hot R&B Songs **chart** in 2017. Khalid then went on a worldwide tour. Every show in the US, Canada, and Europe was sold out.

When the tour ended, Khalid
released his debut album
American Teen. He **embarked**
on his second worldwide tour to
promote the album. Khalid then
opened for Lorde on tour around
the UK.

American Teen was a big
hit. It went platinum by the
Recording Industry Association
of America (RIAA) for selling
more than 1 million albums.

LEGACY

Khalid won the Best New Artist award at the 2017 *MTV Video Music Awards*. He also won the Woodie to Watch award at the *Woodie Awards* that same year.

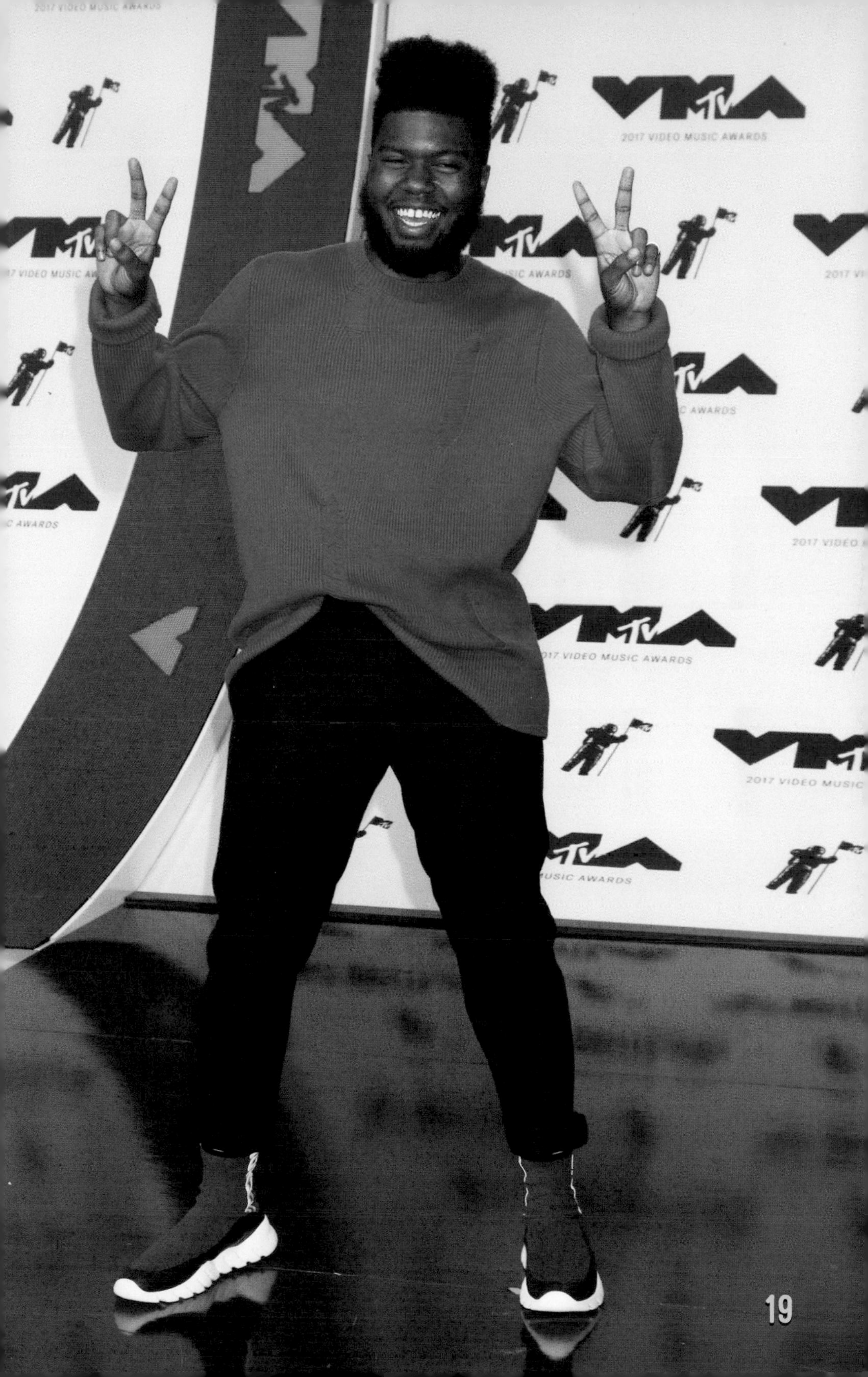
VMA
2017 VIDEO MUSIC AWARDS

In 2018, Khalid was **nominated** for several awards. He took home Top R&B Artist at both the *Billboard Music Awards* and *Teen Choice Awards*.

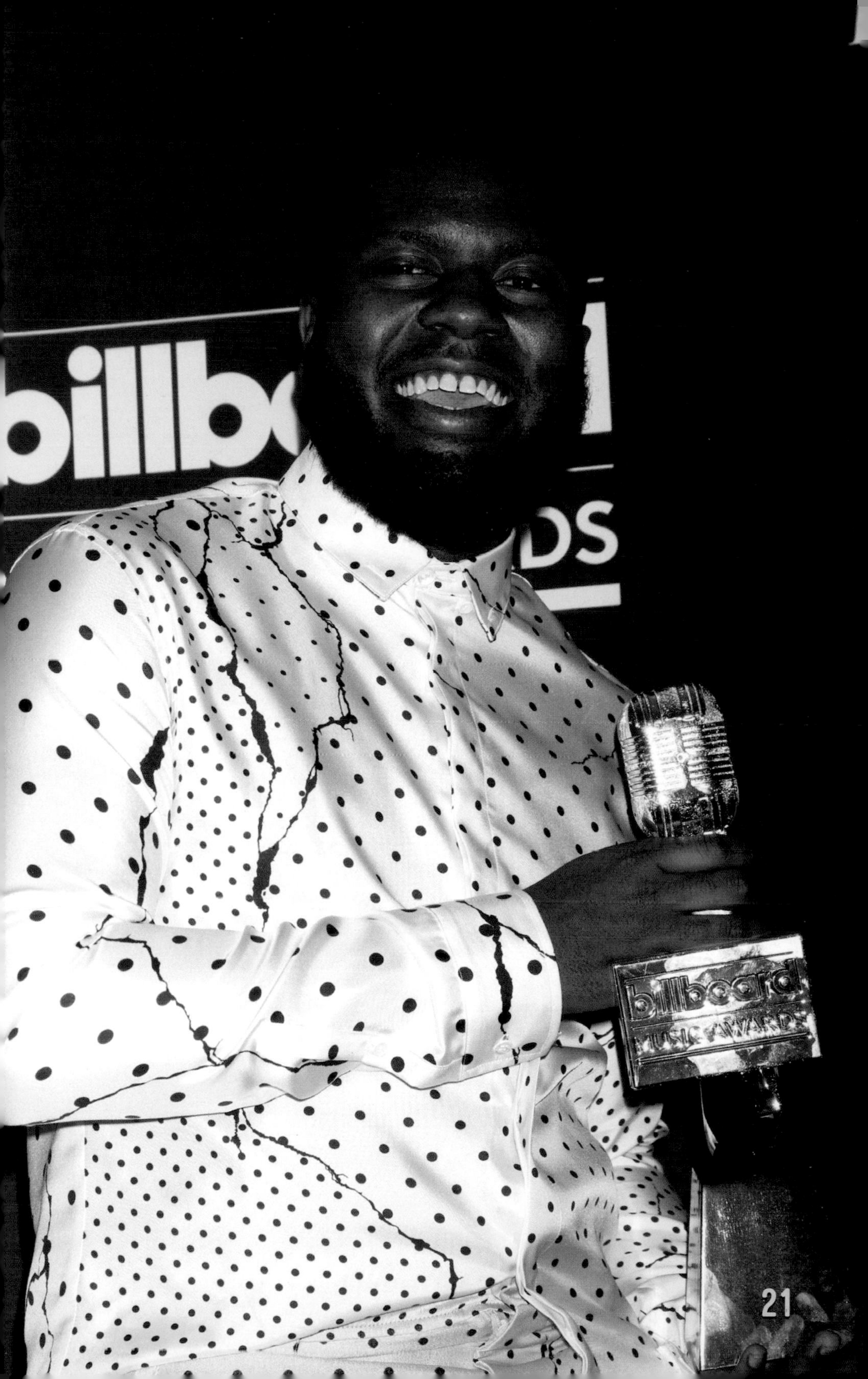
billb
DS
billboard
MUSIC AWARDS

GLOSSARY

chart – a list that shows which music has sold the most during a period of time.

embark – to begin on a journey.

nomination – proposing someone for an honor or award.

prom king – a young man chosen by high school peers to "reign" over prom.

promote – to support and encourage something.

settle – to make a secure spot for a home.

SoundCloud – a music sharing website.

ONLINE RESOURCES

Booklinks
NONFICTION NETWORK
FREE! ONLINE NONFICTION RESOURCES

To learn more about Khalid, please visit **abdobooklinks.com**. These links are routinely monitored and updated to provide the most current information available.

INDEX

American Teen (album) 14, 16

awards 5, 18, 20

Billboard 13, 20

Europe 7, 13, 14

Georgia 6

high school 8, 10

Jenner, Kylie 10

Kentucky 7

Lorde 14

MTV Video Music Awards 18

New York 7

Recording Industry Association of America (RIAA) 16

Teen Choice Awards 20

Texas 8

tour 13, 14

Woodie Awards 18